It's Time to Celebrate

HANUKKAH

Written by
Rebecca Phillips-Bartlett

KidHaven
PUBLISHING

Published in 2026 by
KidHaven Publishing, an Imprint of
Greenhaven Publishing, LLC
2544 Clinton St., Buffalo, NY 14224

Written by: Rebecca Phillips-Bartlett
Edited by: Noah Leatherland
Designed by: Ker Ker Lee

Cataloging-in-Publication Data
Names: Phillips-Bartlett, Rebecca.
Title: Hannukah / Rebecca Phillips-Bartlett.
Description: Buffalo, NY : Kidhaven Publishing, 2026. | Series: Its time to celebrate | Includes index and glossary
Identifiers: ISBN 9781534550124 (pbk) | ISBN 9781534550131 (library bound) | ISBN 9781534550148 (ebook)
Subjects: LCSH: Holidays--Juvenile Literature | Hanukkah—Juvenile Literature
Classification: LCC BM695.H3 P45 2026 | DDC 394.267 --dc25

Manufactured in the United States of America

CPSIA compliance information: Batch #CSKH26
For further information contact Greenhaven Publishing LLC at 1-844-317-7404.

Please visit our website, www.greenhavenpublishing.com.
For a free color catalog of all our high-quality books, call toll free 1-844-317-7404 or fax 1-844-317-7405.

Find us on

Photo Credits – Images are courtesy of Shutterstock.com. With thanks to Getty Images, Thinkstock Photo, and iStockphoto.

Recurring images – MyClipArtStore.com, KanKhem, Artrise Stocker. Cover – KanKhem, PictuLandra, Artrise Stocker, AnastasiiaM. 2–3 – Drazen Zigic. 4–5 – Julia Metkalova, FamVeld. 6–7 – lukpedclub, bilha golan. 8–9 – blueeyes, Fascinadora. 10–11 – Fascinadora, Ksu Shachmeister. 12–13 – Ungvari Attila, StockStudio Aerials, Silver Spiral Arts, SeventyFour. 14–15 – phBodrovaj. 16–17 – Ungvari Attila, StockStudio Aerials, Silver Spiral Arts, SeventyFour. 18–19 – Moti Meiri, Ermak Oksana, TSViPhoto. 20–21 – andreivladpopa, Drazen Zigic. 22–23 – Drazen Zigic, SeventyFour.

Contents

Words that look like <u>this</u> can be found in the glossary on page 24.

It's Hanukkah!

Hi. My name is Asher. My family is Jewish, so we celebrate a festival called Hanukkah. Hanukkah happens in November or December every year.

The exact date of Hanukkah comes from a Jewish calendar which is based on the sun and moon.

Hanukkah celebrates a miracle that happened over 2,000 years ago. The miracle took place across eight days, so Hanukkah celebrations last eight days too. Hanukkah is sometimes known as the Festival of Lights.

The Hanukkah Story

Around 2,200 years ago in Jerusalem, the king wanted everyone to worship Greek gods. Greek armies attacked the Jewish Temple. They broke many important things, including a lamp that burned all day and all night.

A family called the Maccabees fought back. Eventually, the Maccabees and their followers won. They lit the lamp in the Temple again. However, they only had enough oil to burn for one day. Then, a miracle happened. The oil lasted for eight whole days!

Celebrating Hanukkah

During Hanukkah, families meet up to remember and celebrate the miracle that took place. Some families retell the story. Each night, we light a special set of candles on a candlestick known as the menorah.

The Hanukkah menorah is also called a hanukkiah.

Spinning the dreidel is a popular Hanukkah game. Many foods, such as doughnuts and latkes, are eaten at Hanukkah. These foods are fried in oil to remember the oil that kept the lamp burning.

Cooking Corner

Let's Make Latkes

You will need:

- 4 potatoes
- 1 onion
- 2 eggs
- 2 tablespoons (28 g) of plain flour
- Vegetable oil
- Optional: salt and pepper
- A grater
- A frying pan

How to make latkes:

1. Grate your potatoes and onion.
2. Using a tea towel or paper towel, squeeze the grated potatoes and onions dry.
3. Mix together the potatoes, onions, eggs, flour, salt, and pepper in a bowl.
4. Heat some oil in a frying pan.
5. Split the mixture into spoonful-sized pieces.
6. Fry each piece until it is brown.

Graters are sharp. Oil gets very hot. You will need a grown-up to help.

Lighting the Menorah

Every evening during Hanukkah, the Hanukkah menorah is lit. It holds eight candles, plus an extra candle called the shamash. The shamash is lit first and used to light the other candles.

On the first night of Hanukkah, only the shamash and one other candle are lit. Each night, another candle is added. The candles are added from right to left. They are lit from left to right.

Craft Corner

Let's Make a Paper Plate Menorah

You will need:

- A paper plate
- Paper
- Yellow and blue paint
- A paint brush
- Scissors
- Glue

How to make a paper plate menorah:

1. Cut your paper plate in half. Paint one half of the plate yellow.
2. Cut your paper into nine strips. One should be slightly longer than the others.

3. Paint the paper candles blue.
4. Cut nine flames out of paper. Paint these yellow.
5. Once the paint is dry, stick your candles along the flat edge of the paper plate. The longest candle should be in the middle.

This menorah is just for decoration. Do not light your paper menorah!

During Hanukkah

During Hanukkah, we go to the synagogue. At the synagogue, our rabbi tells us the story of the miracle.

After, we make doughnuts called sufganiyot. They are fried in oil. They are very yummy!

In the evening, we play with our dreidel. The dreidel has four sides. On each side, there is a marking. You spin the dreidel and win sweets based on which side is showing.

The markings on the dreidel mean "a great miracle happened here."

Craft Corner

Let's Make a Dreidel

You will need:

- Scissors
- Cardboard – an old cereal box is perfect
- A pencil

How to make a dreidel:

1. Cut out a cardboard square. It should be around 2 inches (5 cm) wide.
2. Draw a line between the opposite corners of the square. It should make a cross in the middle.
3. Draw one of these markings in each section.
4. Stab your pencil into the middle of the square.
5. Use the pencil to spin the dreidel. Where will it land?

Hanukkah Around the World

Hanukkah is celebrated in many countries around the world. People in different countries have their own Hanukkah traditions.

During Hanukkah in Hungary, many rabbis skate on a giant ice rink and light a huge menorah.

During Hanukkah, people used to give money as a gift. However, this tradition changed in the United States. Instead of giving children money, or gelt, people now give out chocolate coins.

It's Time to Celebrate Hanukkah

Now you know all about the Hanukkah miracle and how it is celebrated all over the world. There is one thing left to do. It is time to celebrate Hanukkah!

Have you ever played with a dreidel or made yummy latkes? If not, why not start this year? Each family has their own special Hanukkah traditions. What are yours?

Glossary

festival	a time when people come together to celebrate a special event
miracle	when something happens that cannot be explained
rabbi	a teacher of Judaism
synagogue	a Jewish place of worship
traditions	beliefs and actions that are passed down between people over time

Index